City Maps
Cairo
Egypt

By
James mcFee

© OpenStreetMap contributors
CC BY-SA License

Table Of Contents

Legend

━━━	Motorway	▨	Industrial area	✚	Medical Center
━━━	Main road	▨	Commercial area	👮	Police
- - - -	Track	▨	Heathland	P	Parking
·······	Bridleway	▨	Lake and reservoir	🏫	School
··········	Cycleway	▨	Farm	†	Church
············	Footway	▨	Brownfield site	📮	Post Office
━━━	Railway	▨	Cemetery	📚	Library
━━━	Subway	▨	Allotments	🍽	Restaurant
━━━	Light rail and tram	▨	Sports pitch	🛒	Market
━·━·━	Cable car and chair lift	▨	Sports centre	🍔	Burgers
		▨	Nature reserve	🥤	Drinks
━━━	Airport Runway and taxiway	▨	Military area	🍺	Pub
▨	Airport apron and terminal	▨	School and university	🚲	Bicycle Parking
		■	Significant building	👕	Clothing
───	Administrative boundary	▪	Railway station	🏋	Gym
▨	Forest	▲	Summit and peak	🏃	Track
▨	Wood	······	Dashed casing = tunnel	🏛	Museum
▨	Golf course	═══	Black casing = bridge	🏦	Bank
▨	Park	- -	Private access	🚁	Helipad
▨	Residential area	- -	Destination access	🐾	Pet Store
▨	Common and meadow	▨	Roads under construction	📱	Electronics Store
▨	Retail area			💎	Jewelry Store
				☕	Coffee Shop
				🏨	Hotel

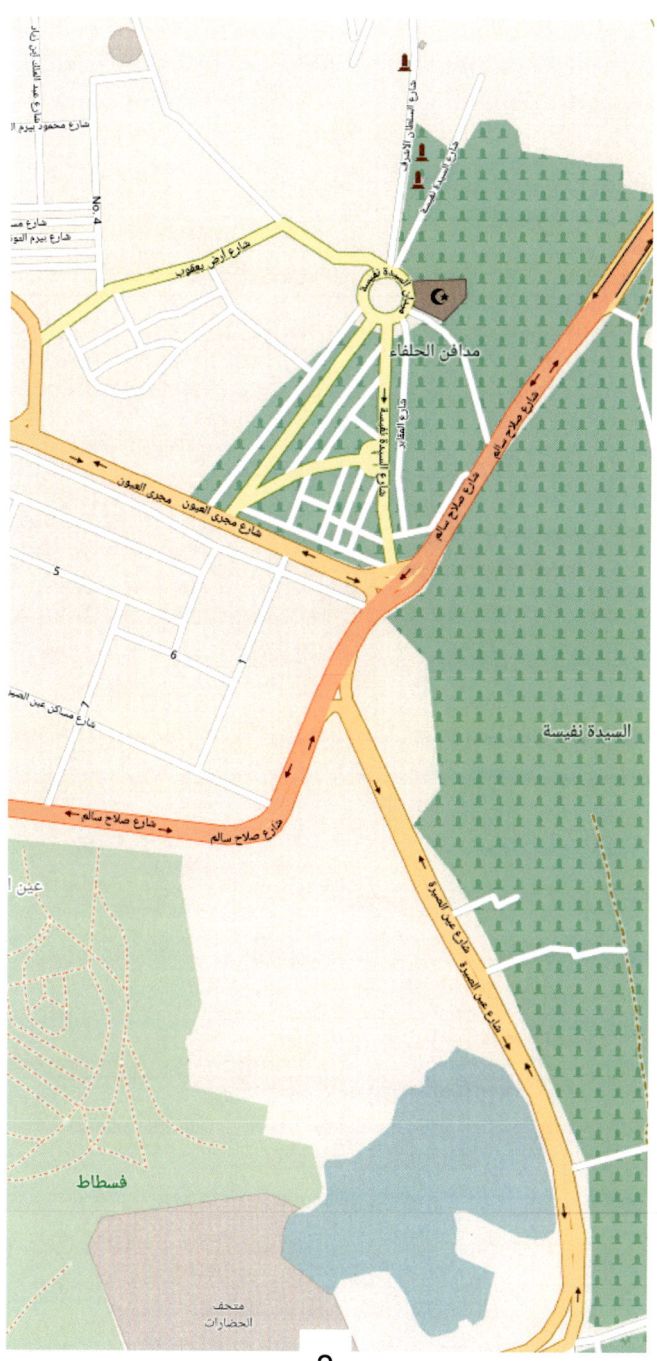

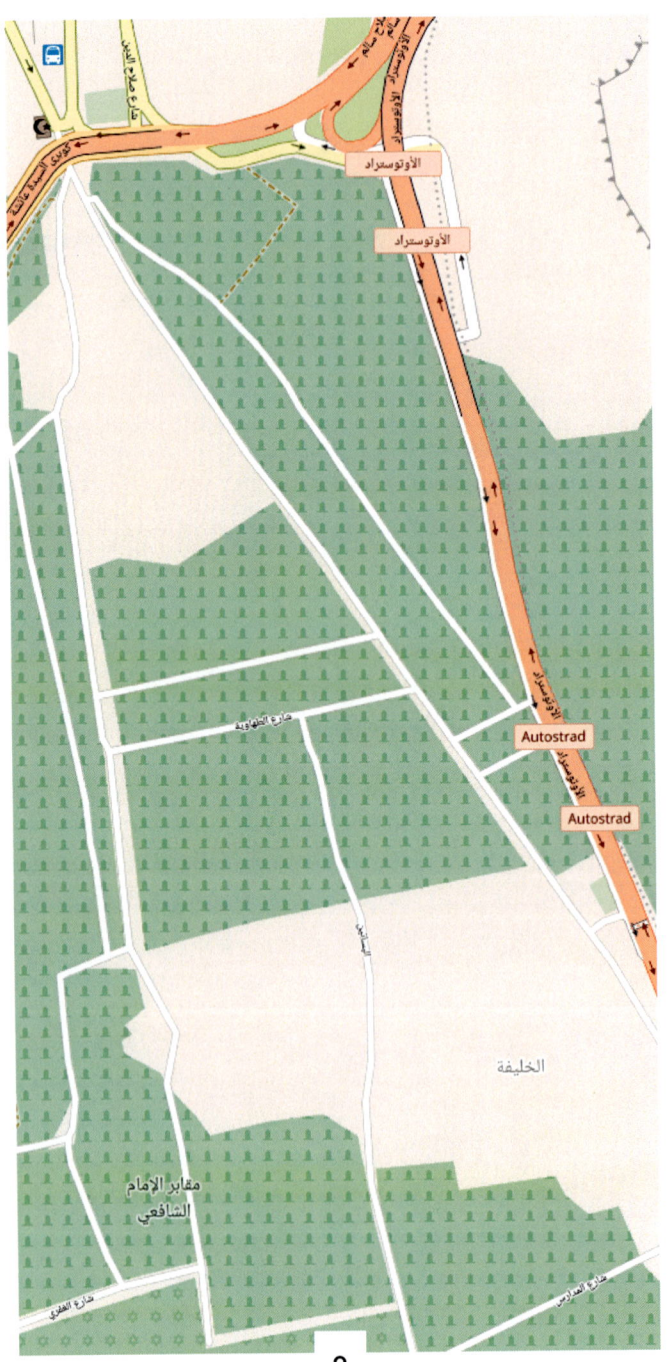

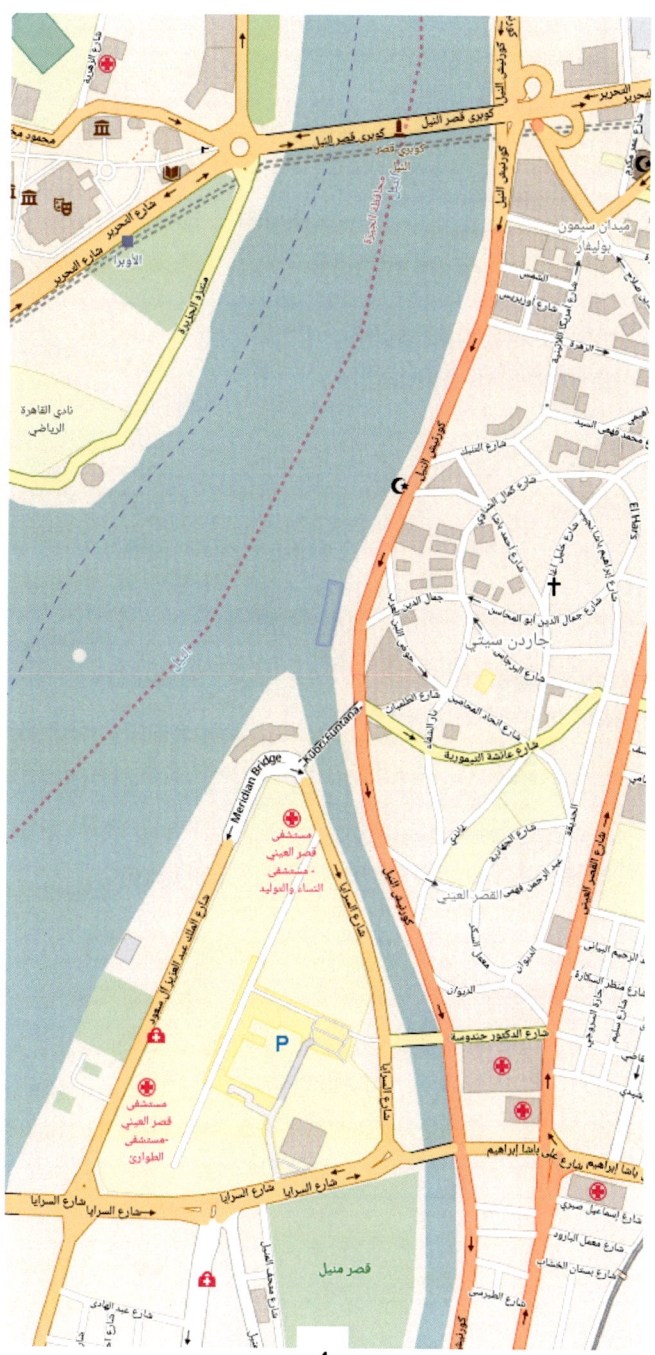

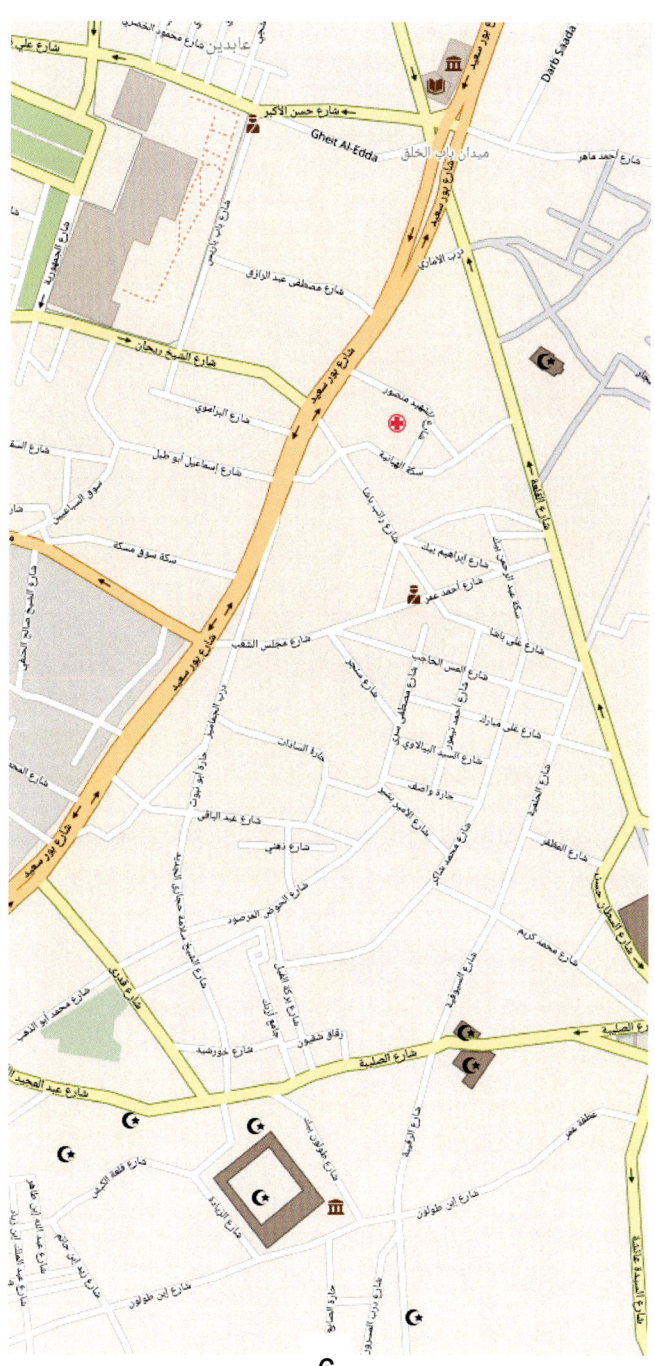

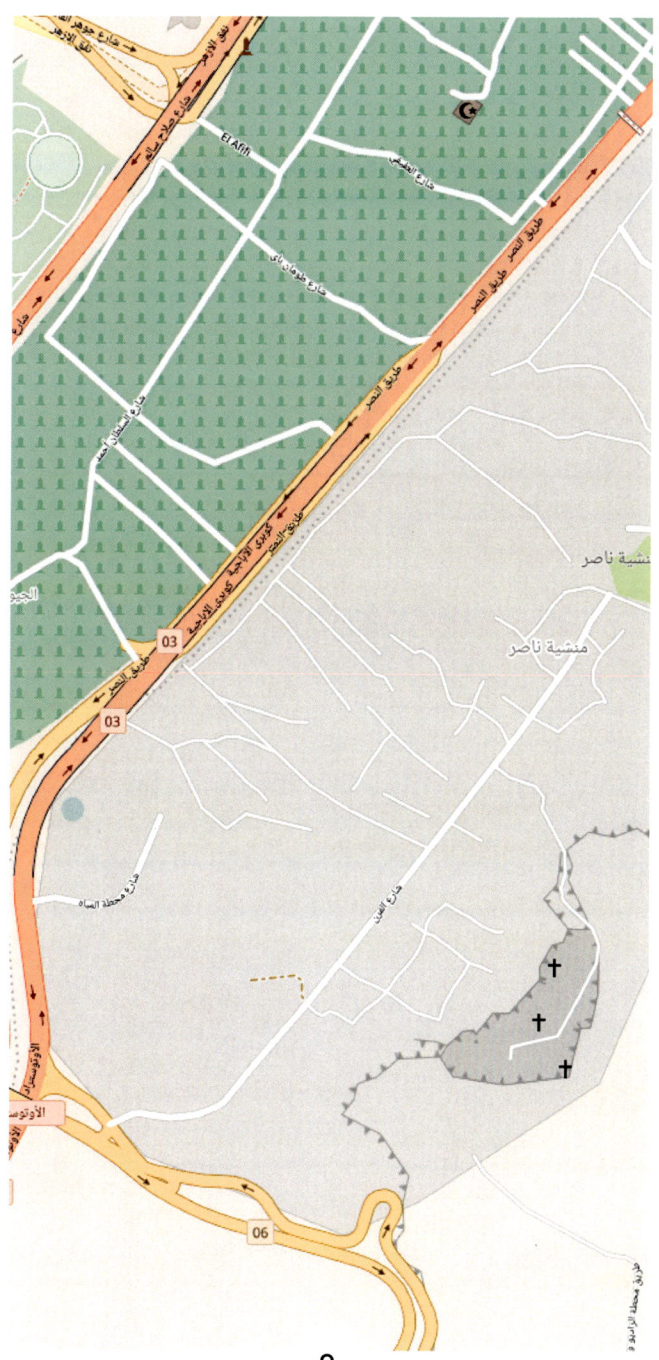

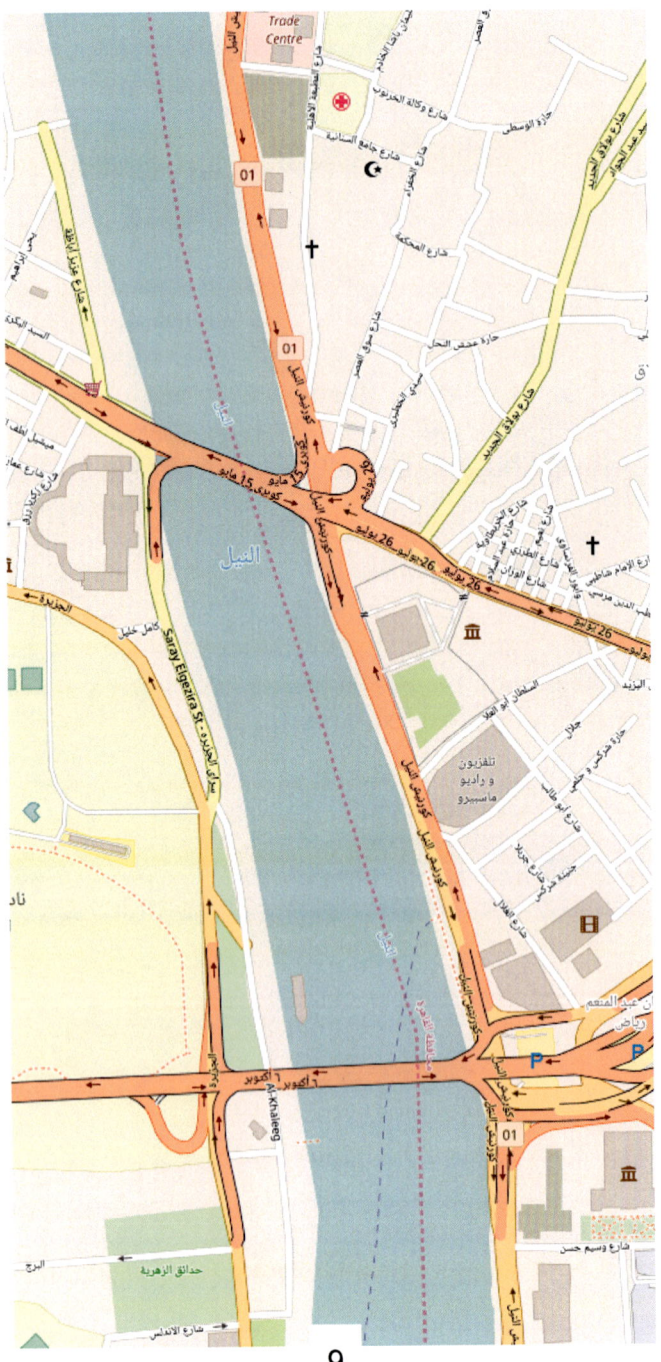

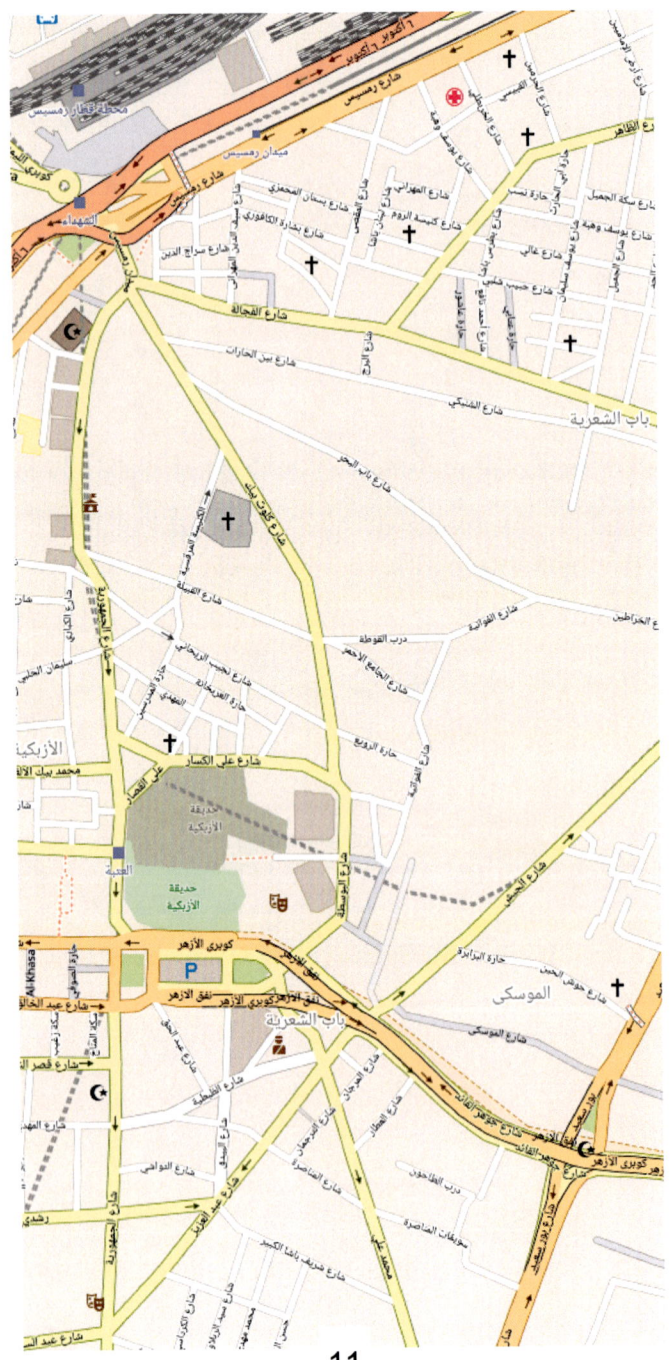

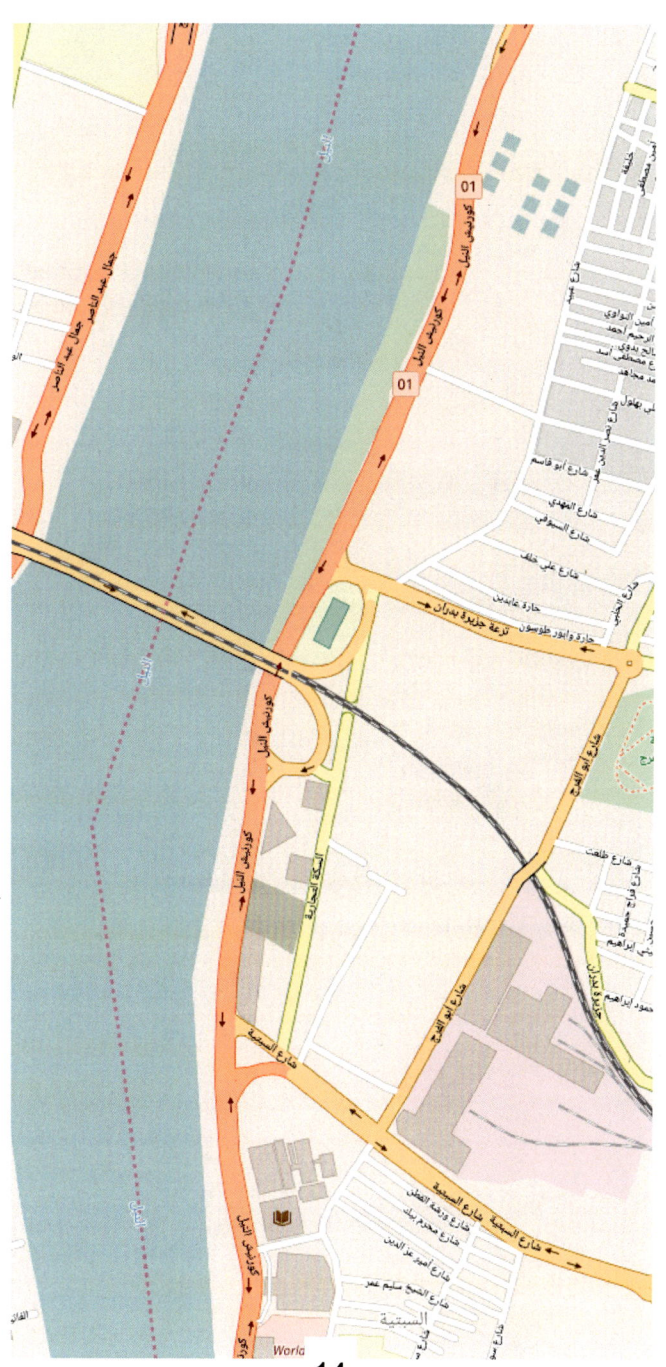

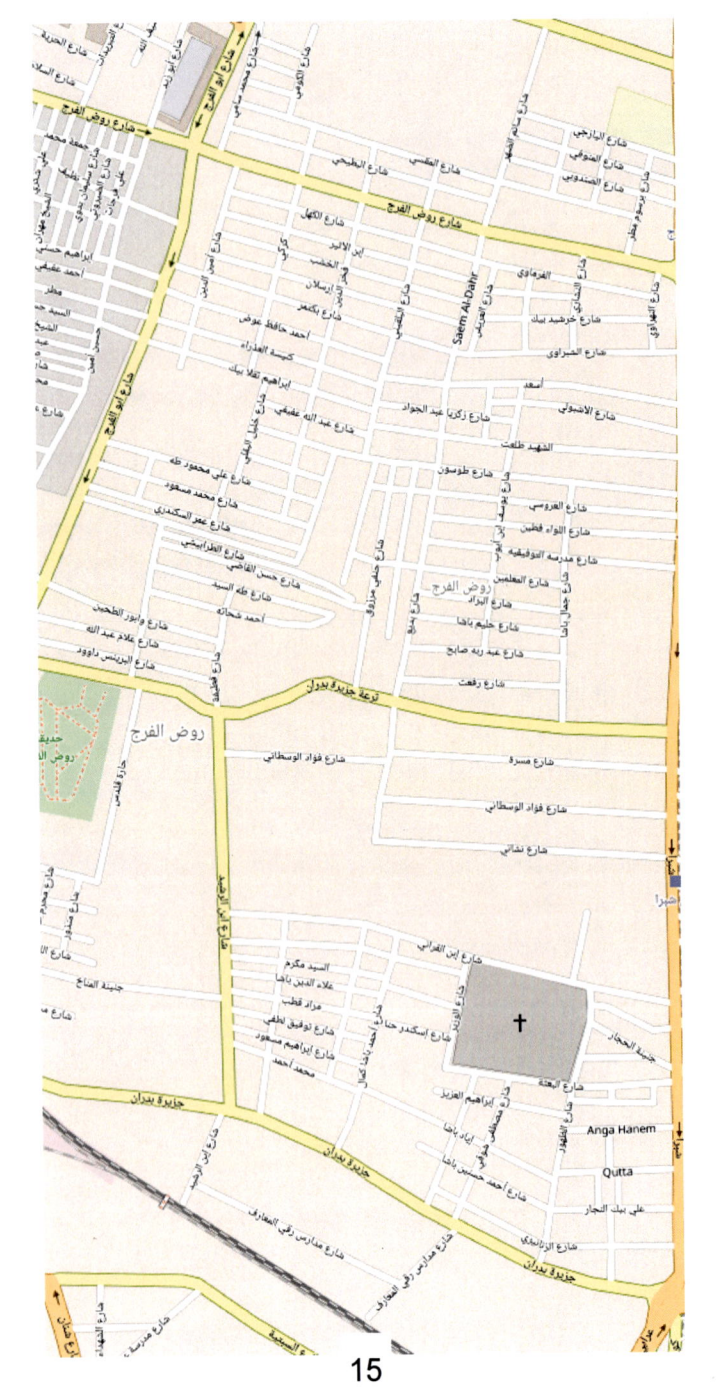

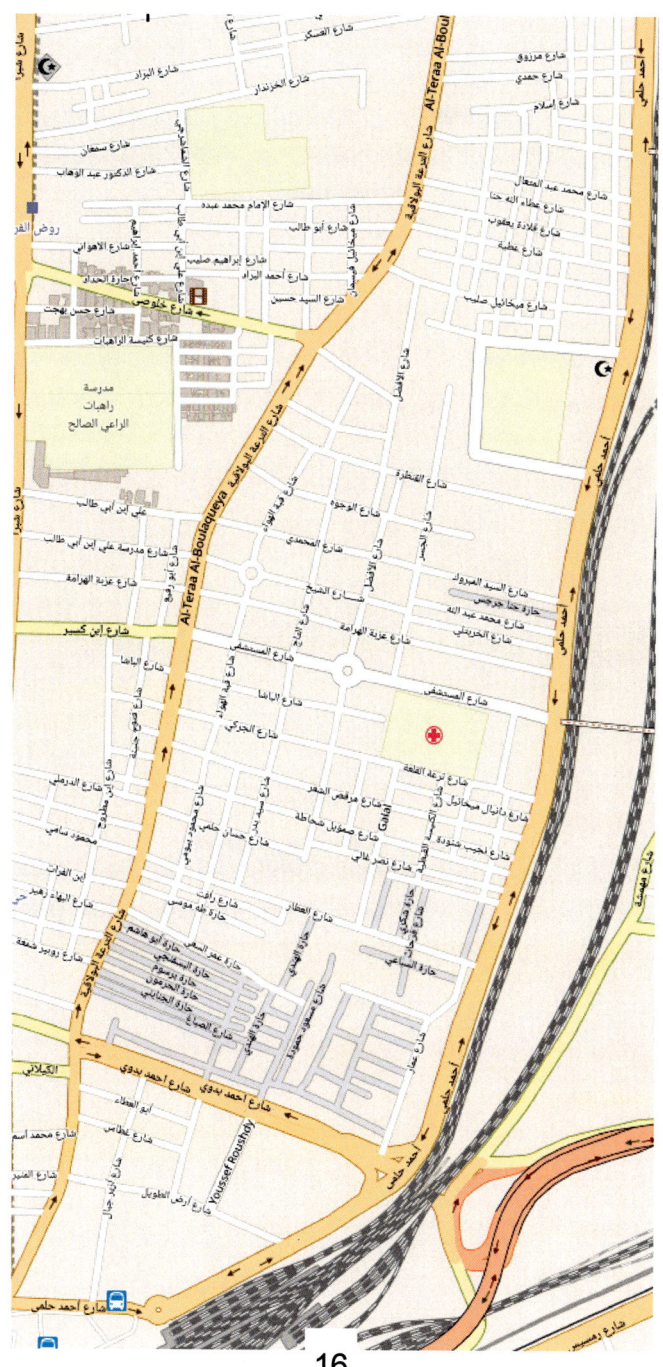

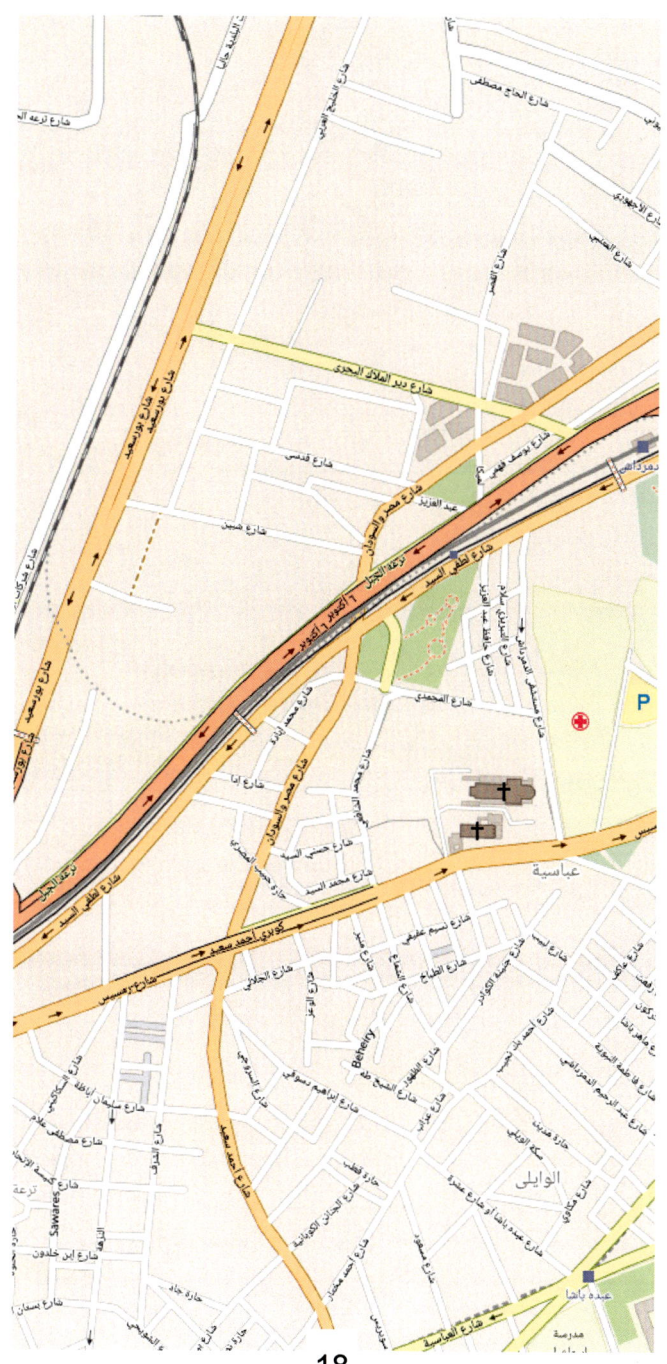

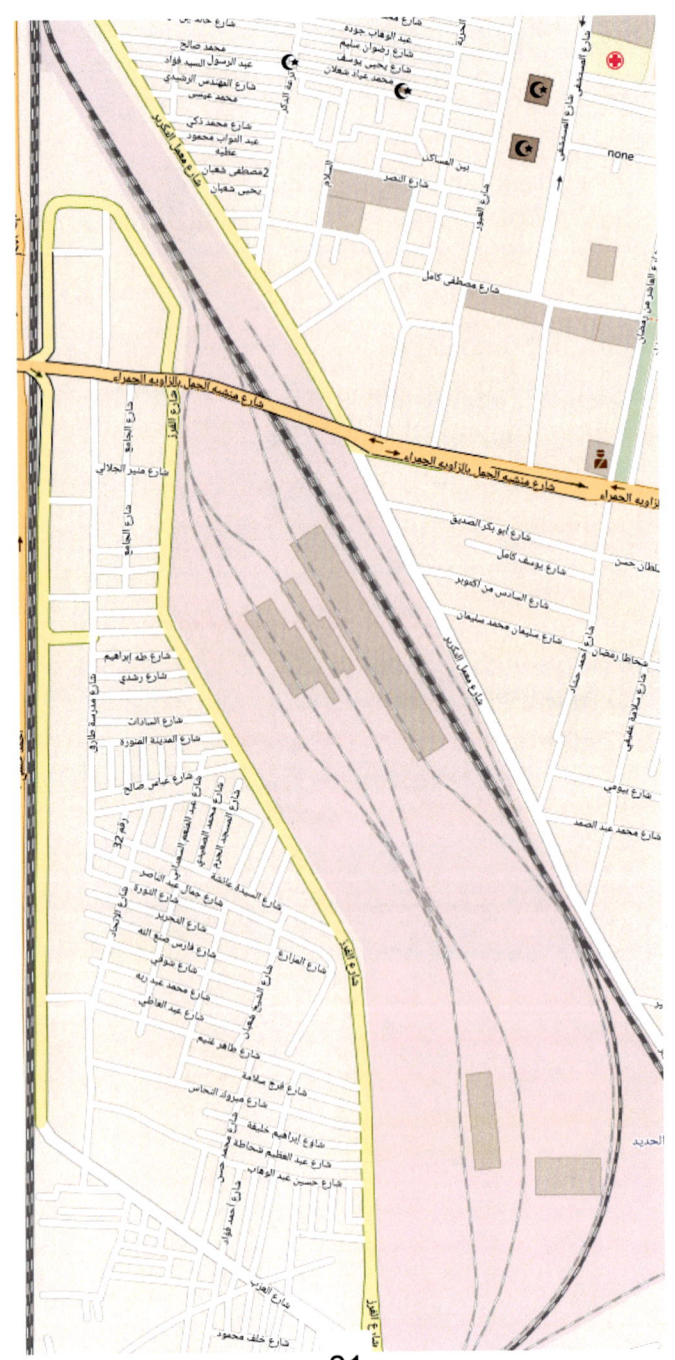

Made in the USA
Lexington, KY
24 September 2018